D1096116

Diamonds
Only Water Can Wear

The poetry of
Aaron Silverberg

Diamonds Only Water Can Wear
© 2007 Aaron Silverberg

All Rights reserved. No part of this book may be used or reproduced in any form or by any electronic or mechanical means , including storage and retrieval systems without written permission in writing from the publisher, except for brief quotations to be used in reviews and articles.

Off the Map Enterprises
Seattle Washington

First Edition

Library of Congress Cataloging-in-Publication Data
ISBN 978-1-4243-3635-7

Produced / Edited / Designed
by PA Ellinghausen / Seattle Empress
Printed and bound in the USA

Diamonds
Only Water Can Wear

For Bo,

Thanks for being green!

Aaron

12/18/18

The poetry of
Aaron Silverberg

Off The Map Enterprises
Seattle 2007

For Uncle Hermy

Contents

Foreword

What good fortune to hear the power of Aaron
Silverberg's poems in a cozy North Seattle lounge, under
the peaceful smile of a giant Buddha.

There is a reliability in his voice that reassures me about the
whole enterprise of poetry.

Aaron's poems extend a generous offer of companionship.

I believe Aaron poetry heals in a similar spirit as Rilke, Bly
and Rumi.

"Diamonds Only Water Can Wear", like Aaron's first book,
"Thoreau's Chair", is transcendental in its vision. Transcendental, as Emerson first meant it, to make God more acces-
sible through a direct experience of nature and spirit.

To enliven and expand your experience, take liberties
repeating lines, stanzas, and even whole passages as many
times as necessary (as Aaron himself does during readings)
to crack through the words to the vital energies, touching
upon new levels of awareness and understanding. This join-
ing with your larger nature, your "infinite being" is where
Aaron guides you.

These are heart songs, vignettes humbly shared and joyfully sung. These songs belong to conscious beings who are
striving to co-create Paradise.

Dear reader, may you to take these poems into your heart.

Jed Myers, *Raconteur*
Seattle, WA

**Diamonds
Only Water Can Wear**

Go lightly, know the flowers, stay together.

~Gary Snyder

Solace

Yes
it would be lovely
to hold the wren

for a moment,

feel the softness of its wings,
the staccato of its heart,

but it is better
that it sings
                    yonder.

Dedication

She walks out in the morning
barefoot,
each fist full of a different
colored chalk.

She reaches the property line,
mixture of brick and dung and
Ganges rainwater.

She pours the chalks,
weaving past and present
into an intricate knot.

She admires her handiwork,
claps her hands so sharply
magpies take flight.

Through the monsoon heat,
children, cripples, dogs, chickens, oxen
trample the chalks
back into tea-colored earth.

Next morning she will rise
with the mango sun
and pour the chalks again.

Impossible to Choose

Which is more loving,

doula
who welcomes
sloshing baby,

or

reaper
who severs raspy breather
from tattered body?

Coming in, going out.

Each swaying
        bowing
                bough,
a child's hand,
waving
hello and goodbye.

Etched

Central Indiana,
nighttime,
driving the interstate northbound,
muscles sore from climbing hills
in Brown County.

October full moon
fat and flush in the sky.

Suddenly we pass an open field
and there it is,
oak tree perfection.

Silhouetted in silver light
every gnarly,
        gilded,
            intricate
aspect of its bearing
cast out.

I dragged that oak
by its humongous roots
in my fist-sized heart
for twenty years.

Slowly,
over time,
it etched
each
nobly
curved
branch,

inside mine.

Slow motion

Snowflakes fall
the way love
rises,

meeting somewhere
between the lamp light
and my heart.

A little girl peeks
out the window,
to see if I like
her snowman.

Incantations

Dimpled clouds cling to the sky
like hammered pockmarks
to your pewter mug.

Small children mutter
to themselves
in the next yard.

Airplanes drone
like thunder that can't find
the ground.

You are here,
somewhere,
smiling in the brown grass.

Lifetime in Paris

I sat down to rest in the Tuilleries,
the gardens out back of the Louvre,
where I had tramped for five hours,
nonplussed by the glassed and glary "Mona Lisa."

A dignified Parisian matron sat next to me,
proudly overseeing her eight year old
granddaughter.

The little girl's antics,
gave me a tangible joy
gaudy furniture and gilded art,
could not impart.

The grandmother turned to me,
aware of our mutual delight
and said,
"You must be French!"

Luneria

Unusual weed
grows in my garden,
paper circles on a
miniature tree.

Taken inside,
each unwrapped coin,
a silken treasure.

People,
exposed to the elements,
have this rough layer too.

Everyone, everything
peeled with kindness
reveals a similar sheen.

Stay

Why are you rushing,
always rushing
like some panic struck wind
fleeing across a forgotten lake?

Lay down on that
chilling white ice,
under the blinding sun.

Let the wind pass.

Cry,
until the ice surrenders,
until you recall the warm sea,
until your destination
is where you are.

Heaven

Laying in tall grass,
end of a summer day,
flies in mid-air
               genuflecting.

Culture Change

Strolling the inner deck of the ferry
M/V Klahowya,
Chinook for Greetings.

I stop to inspect
black and white photos of the native "Ish" people.[1]

They look slight, sad, and tired.

They sit,
facing the Sound,
awkward in White Man's clothes.

There is resignation in their eyes,
like wild animals,
exiled from their own habitat.

Along the shore,
racks of split salmon,
hand built cedar canoes,
stained hands that know subsistence.

What have we learned from these people,
other than contrived words
put in Chief Sealths' bewildered mouth?

How impoverished we are,
relying on technology,
instead of a lineage of skillfulness.

Who will photograph us
when we are conquered
as mercilessly?

Where the Ant Goes

Do you remember how hard it was
to crush an ant?

You would press your finger with all your might
and backing off slowly
discover a miracle of movement.

Bending down,
unsure exactly how to kiss those microscopic
steel-clamped jaws,
you would press onward
your force of death
undoing the miracle.

But when the ant was vanquished for good,
you wanted to follow its tiny soul,
backwards
        forwards
                sideways

however it made its way
to the place
you cannot press,
        cannot touch,
        cannot hold
        tenderly
                in your troubled hand.

No Such Thing

There is no such thing as
love,
only this feeling
in the belly,
in the groin,
in the flush of face.

She said,
"it'd be easier to kiss you
than tell you about this fear inside,
easier to get smashed by a goddamned comet
than be this vulnerable."

Bobby Hull's Third Palm

On long, frigid nights
he massaged oils and unguents
into the thirsty pine,
coaxing the slight curvature
rounder and rounder,
singing songs he'd never heard,
moaning like North Ontario gusts,
howling wolf,
Athabaskan shaman.

Miraculously, wooden blade softens,
into the suppleness of a hand.

Even taped, Bobby could feel the flex of his
third palm.

That night, Stan Makita dances across the Blue line,
a writhing cobra
deftly slithering around defenders.

Left wing rushes to smother Stans' charge.
At the last moment he flicks the puck backwards,
tumbling into Bobby's sickle,
he spots it.

For the merest fraction of time
the puck stands alone,
a lonely shred of charcoal.

Then Bobby snaps out enchanted wood
and liquid rock,
loosed from David's sling,
spins aloft,
puncturing the net,
goalie hopelessly contorted.

Red light lit,
the Madison crowd
erupts into bedlam.

Red-cheeked Bobby grins the grin,
raises the blade and
kisses his creation.[2]

Turkey Fig

Large and bulbous when ripe,

inside
succulent flesh,
a world unequivocally
tender.

Subtle sweetness tinged with the tropical,

pink, purple, puckered and dense,

unmistakably vulval.

Yet the majesty of engorgement,
from reticent green to
striated honker,
decidedly male.

Partaking of such swollen abundance,
Adam and Eve
didn't bother with leaves.

Victory

At 11-12 in the third set tie-breaker
euphoria came over me.

The fear of losing,
slipped down
the long rock face.

I won at 24-22,
after saving a dozen match points,
like McEnroe's miracle against Borg.

The rest of my life
I have striven for that same,
Providential peace.

Umptanum Canyon

Prairie falcon chicks
tumble over each other
in a tiny cave
500 feet up the cliff side.

Sage fills the air.

Aspen quakes.

Turkey vulture swoops down the ridge line

Lazuli bunting,
Chat,
Goldfinch,
Grosbeak,
swap perches.

Swallows sweep over the Yakima river.

Harmlessness

Rising and falling of the cat's belly.

Tiny ears of dew
nab murmurings of worms
and morning beetles.

Heron's wings lazily leave their loft.

Face of a sleeping son,
lights lit,
books and drawings scattered.

History

Heave of the great boat,
oars churning in unison.

Steel on steel,
thousands upon thousands
of sandaled feet.

Burning crops,
sobbing mothers,
dazed children.

In the distant hills,
                        goat bells.

Flip of a Coin

This is not
desolation.

This is not
torture.

This is privilege, entitlement, cush.

This is the sound of silver
spinning
between kindness and rage.

World Domination

Trekking the dry foothills
between Chang Mai and Burma.[3]

A cup of packed rice,
a few swallows of tepid tea,
a steep narrow path
for my oversized, Western feet.

Porters joke and smile,
carrying twice my load.

Each frigid night
a thin bamboo mat
separates the animal kingdoms.

Below me roosters crow
all night long.

In the middle of the sweltering day
I nap.
Stir-fry, incense and opium smoke
curls in the rafters.

As I stride out of the Lahu village,
a little girl reaches out
and touches my beard.

Moth and the Flame

Each human being is a moth and a candle flame.

Circling and dying,
circling and dying,
circling and dying.

No choice but to become one
With the source of Love.

This idea of celestial freedom,
        dipping in the flame and
        flying free,
a fallacy,
we sometimes call "democracy".

The moth gives everything
to be the flame.

Permit me to gaze
at a world
where candles fly
and moths burn radiant and true.

In Case of Emergency

Tune in for further instructions
Move to higher ground.

Check your sources.
Be prepared for anything.
Carry a clean hanky.

Forget the coupons.
Wait 'till you see the whites of their eyes.
Pull tab and tear on the dotted line.
Consult local authorities.

Ask for a complete refund.
Proceed to staging area C4.
Demand a recount.
Follow the lighted arrows.
Cash in your chips.

Leave it to beaver.

Fritter

In less than a billion years
the Earth will be uninhabitable.

The aging sun will have steamed off
the polar ice caps,
the air will be like Venus soup.

Let the Chinese burn the coal,
the French blow up
perfectly good atolls.

Loiter a little,
with someone you love.

Fritter away a few hours with sidewalk chalk.

Listen to some elders'
disappearing
story.

Working the Craft

Taste the onomatopoeia of
      Insurgency.

"in-surge-we-see"?

Dionysian
pathos
dried into
pathetic.

While Pan loitered on our tongue,
muck
feather
swollen
purr
tart.

Abounding in the magnanimous gesticulations
of a five year old
rapt in wet sand.

Absolutely

Kissing her fingertips,
Parisian gas lamps flicker.

An accordion plays and
stops.

A bead of sweat hovers
above the Sphinx' lips.

This is why willows
hang
so close to the pond.

Where Buddhists Come From

Parade me again
       downwind
honeysuckle blossom,
unabashed
by your fragrance.

Yes, smile in the lotus position.

Three hundred arms and legs,
thrashing equanimity,
molten hara,
crimson face,

"be the fuckin' Buddha"
"be the fuckin' Buddha"
"BE   THE   FUCKING   BUDDHA"!!!

Plum Wisdom

Don't get stuck trying to choose
a single plum.

Put them all in your mouth!

They are all me.

Crisp

We are
scars across a whales'
belly,

ribs of sand
abandoned by the morning tide,

ripe apples
bobbing
in the forgiving sea.

Giftwrapping

Upon my desk
a brightly wrapped box.

Little card reads,
"For the Beloved"
"From the Beloved"
and
"Never to be opened!"

Every friend is such a gift.

On cruel days
I wish I carried shiny paper
to wrap the frightened child staring out the bus window,
the retired man walking his dogs, with frozen face,
the Eastern European woman trudging past
the refugee camp of her childhood.

It's not just poverty,
illness or death I struggle against,
it's the gleaming colors,
the dangling ribbon,
the mysterious anticipation
that can never be put in a box.

A Revolution of Simplicity

They're traded their SUVs
for hammocks.

Instead of sipping Starbucks,
they're giving hugs and foot rubs.

They've killed their TV sets
to sit in meditation
with the pain of their own
neglect.

They're dancing and sweating,
pouring into each others eyes.[4]

Bewilderment

Love soaked bodies

like pound-cake
dunked in milk,

saturated
to the surrender point.

Candle Time

Tinges of ochre, sienna, crimson
stain the sunny side of maples.

Slight tang in the air
that crows and squirrels scavenge.

Pumpkins lie pregnant
on porches,

ghouls dangle in doorways,

rosehips, bruised and blackened,
linger.

Storytellers warm up their stories.

Enticements

Purple dusk,
campfire coals aglow,

my flute serenades
twenty spent paddlers
sprawled across the sandbar.

Smoke wafts,

sparks fly,

Wisconsin river slumbers on.

Intergalactic Ravish

Each night the gods
slip off their clothes,
step into a bath
of milky star shine.

Moon-seduced waves
lap in understated praise.

Frogs and a gazillion crickets
rub body parts into ecstatic song.

The tears of a glacier plunk
hollow
into a deep crevasse.

And in some far away galaxy,
plasma dances like a
possessed belly-dancer,
lit up with the electric semen
of the ten-thousand lovers
that would ravish her.

Enlightenment

came and you
remained

Agitation vacated.

The idea of future or past
became ridiculously funny.

Slums and penthouses
looked curiously alike.

You lost your appetite for
acquisitions.

Job, lover, retirement account
became
thicket of ripe berries, resplendent sunset,
children singing.

The whole world
grasped,
as a gypsy's palm
around yours.

Look Again

The world is a trick birthday candle,
blown out,
it relights itself.

Same view out the same window,
same collection of oddly-placed trees,
power lines,
same moss covered stones
huddled under
same mailboxes.

Each day I wake to this sorry cast of characters,
Trying to direct a Broadway smash.

Look again.
It's as fresh today
a packed house,

Haphazard splay of
apple branches,

enshrouding mist of
cedar and fir,

The candle keeps lighting
'cause a birthday is never over.
the celebration never dims.

Dharma Inquiry

If you found a wish-fulfilling jewel

would you use it,

sell it,

give it away,

or destroy it?

Fulfillments

Holding hands,
wandering off the path,
calling back to the loons.

Skinny dipping,
soaking in a hot spring,
sparks spinning off a campfire.

Kissing eyelids,
skipping stones,
scattering the wishes of a dandelion.

Brushing a lovers cheek,
undressing,
receiving the Beloveds'
unexpected gifts.

Reassurances

I grew old along Skookum Flats [5]
frozen with entanglements.

Each breath of the river
glances dark and light.

A kingfisher slips downstream,
a brief chuckle
and he's out of sight.

Inland Sea

Someday we will cry
an inland sea.

Lovely creatures
will flock there,
float their troubles away.

On its dazzling surface,
dancing with abandon,
diamonds only water can wear.

No Offense

Forget diets,
forget grandiose pilgrimages,
forget tantric sex and the bliss navel
of the Universe.

See how long you can go
without being offended.

Middle Eastern Peace Plan

Arab and Jew serve each other
impeccably,
wash each others feet,
marry each others sons and daughters,
share each others profits and losses.

Each day sitting
with each others
terror and shame.

No one knows what music plays
on the other side of the doorway.

Why fight over tickets that may not
be honored?

Together,
greeting our naked maker,
huddling in the muddy banks
of the Jordan river,
waiting for the stones,
the bullets,
the bulldozers,
to stop pretending,
there are enemies

in the Holy Land.

Miracle in Montana

Flying to Kalispell
to meet my blood sister,
first time
at age 41.

The plane,
sleek, comfortable Fokker,
built by caring Germans,
some peculiar irony
since my sister and I
were Jewish orphans,
given up by a mother
traumatized in America
by Holocaust fallout.

Outside the aircraft,
clouds billow thickly,
draping majestic mountains,
gleaming green and gold.

Out this stupendous window,
no traces of blood, wailing ... death.

Part of me refuses.

It shouldn't have happened.

My sister and I laugh, cry and
rest,
touching noses.

What People?

I never shot an arrow
clean through
a poised buck.

Moment of truth,
reciting multiplication tables,
war hero of Middle Earth.

My father learned of revolution in
sweat-drenched books,
throwing jabs at phantom foes,
boxing an enemy
he would never meet.

No comrades sat in our living room,
they languished
in Spanish poetry books,
smoking Galoise and
cursing the lack of unity
in Barcelona.

My parents were Maranos,
secret Jews who didn't practice,

secret slaves
to hidden overlords,
tiny modernized shtetl,
minus village extras, chickens ... goats.

God flew away
in the ash and soot
of Berkenwald, Auschwitz, Triblenka

What remained?
An obsession with survival
and enduring love.

Deeper than Marrow

Stand-up bass player
hovers and thrums
rifs so low
your bones rumble

Godflesh

There is continuity
beyond fingertips and toes,

waters lapping
a salmon carcass,

winds shredding prayer flags,

braille landscape
left in lava's
blind surges,

inside quivering circle
where
tiny clear skin
of raindrop
bursts.

Christmas Offering

Serenity is here,

cobwebs bask in it,

stands next to you
as gas tank fills,

lays along sidewalks,

nestles in your bedsheets

rests on the cats' eyelids,

whispers lullabies,

remains
when you depart.

Into the Dark

Not only Orpheus
descends,
to reclaim
lost love.

Each winter solstice,
mother earth
torn from the heart of father sun,
abides in black radiance.

Om tara tutare ture soha.[6]

Nature

Smell like a coyote
Hear like a deer
Touch like a slug
Lay like a meadow
Dream like a desert
Smile like a monkey
Swaggle like a shark
Sing like a whale
Burrow like a badger
Camouflage like a salamander
Nap like a lion
Swim like a seal
Build like a beaver
Kick like a kangaroo
Chew like a buffalo
Swing like an orangutan
Howl like a wolf
Dangle like a spider
Play like a dolphin
Wade like a moose
Leap like a salmon
Pounce like a puma
Hover like a heron

See like an eagle
Taste like a rabbit
Think like a mountain
Speak like an elephant
Dance like a crane
Jump like a springbok
Sun like a turtle
Blink like an owl
Float like an otter
Parade like a peacock
Soar like an albatross
Bound like a fox
Hang like a bat
Plummet like a falcon
Preen like a swan
Romp like a bear
Hide like a crab
Scavenge like a crow
Wallow like a hippo
Hop like a frog
Cheer like a river
Stare like a lemur
Strut like a giraffe

laugh and cry like you.

Patois

I don't care for pate,
way too dry and reminiscent
of the dreaded liver
my mother tried to sell me on.

I'd rather chew on patois,
sing-song ditty
flung along a musty cobble,

street vendors miserable
in Port-au-Prince,

swaying hips and third world colors.

Mustering courage,
I parade my Seattle streets,
be-bopping and scatting,
tapping and morse-coding,
slapping down ju-ju rifs like
wet mortar,
for the way I feel
now.

Profusion

Salmon poppies dangle their petticoats,
peaflowers tumble,
velvet iris hangdogs,
hundreds of fuzzy peachettes stringle,
red roses unfurl floosies,
kale leaves fatten,
carrot tops shimmy,
green figs probiscuate,
potato leaves flapple,
proud strawberry mothers parasol
yellow-green seedcoats
and
bees bumble in the
blue blazing ceanothus.

Cry of the Yeti

Orange-red trees
smolder
under a streetlamp.

Leaves shuffle,
drains gurgle,

wind catches in stupa's curl.

Shadows
unhurried as Himalayan pilgrims,
circle Kailas.

Lady Macbeths' Hands

Desert winds
scatter gold dust and sand
with equal joy.

The Madonna of Frisco

Walking down Market Street,
restless as the city itself,
immune to panhandlers and prostitutes,
trashy storefronts,
telltale transience.

Adrenaline loneliness
impaling dark underbelly
of sunny Cal-i-forn-i-a.

Electronic funds are whisked to the 'burbs,
where junior and missy scowl
in the back of a Volvo.

I, dart in the shadows,
tie askew, my suburban marriage
unraveling like a cheap sweater.

At the end of my emotional rope, I freeze.

Above
a huge statue of working class people,
glinting in sodium light.

Below, cradled in street bench,
beautiful black woman,
slumbering street angel,
union of bronze and ebony

Relationship Fire Escape

Everyone has one if not many
travelers' cheques smashed into a wallet's
crease,
condom too.

Spare lover,
friend who listens,
therapist,
some little shack where you can
hole up,
clear your dang-fool head.

A little plan Stan.
Buddies who cut you slack,
misogyny,
"yea, I threw her back, plenty more
fish where that came from."

Workaholism,
date of the month club,
no follow up calls.

Sleep with someone else,
fill your basement with resentments

and take out flood insurance.

Find someone more available, present, attentive.

Start over fresh,
page ripped out of typewriter,
crumpled and chucked.

The relationship fire escape
is just outside your emergency backdoor.

When you swing the bulky thing over,
clang down those rickety black iron steps,

you're standing
in the very same fire
you thought you outran.

No Soliloquy

I am never alone
in Gaia's garden.

Trembling with leaves,
summoned by birdsong,
stunned by the purpleblack coat of
the beetle,
staggering from the depths.

Gooey

There is a whisper
I strain
to hear,

Along the empty road

Sweetness carries me
in its side pocket
like melted chocolate.

Is there

a chance we'll meet
again?

Linger like a teardrop
in the corner of an eye.

Smile like Buddhas
blessing the ages.

Press together
like leaves between
anonymous pages.

First Candy

An old man sits on a bench
alongside other old men.

They watch
a crinkly leaf
dance in a circle,
scraping ground,
like their canes,
like their tap shoes
dragged long ago.

A great wind gathers at their feet,
spins old men and bench,
aloft,
like first balloon
each let go as a boy.

Rising into New York sky,
dentures grin
gets dimmer.

Ten million arms
wave together,
like forests,
like flocks taking flight,

like your grandfathers' first peppermint,
thrown into your mouth.

Skagit Summons

We paddled our kayak through the shallow
tideflats,

where the Stilliguamish
        rushes to kiss
                its salty mother.

Coming round
        a small bend,

rising in slow motion,
        nine white angels,
                plump bodies,
                        humped harlequin masks,
their throaty call
an invitation,
        to rub wonder from our
                rock skimming eyes.

Trumpeter swans,
they are called by laymen,
but their effortful flight,
hovering on the edge of stalling,
made me dub them summoner swans.

          up,
      me
Calling

     the still morning air,
   into
up

above

the salmonberry, [7]
struggling,
to choose itself
       a color.

Spun

Yes, you are all pink
 inside.

As my tautological tongue,
torrents and testifies,
        spinning and swirling,
twirling and conspiring,

        bejeweled with a dervish effervescence,

        sparkly filaments
        floating   to the side.

        My paper cone is bushily full
and your tongue tastes it
with tortoise-like integrity.

Sephardic serenade of mutinous slugs,
lapping the prickly-sweets,
disappearing and reappearing
        like the magic breath that
utters,

"cotton candy."

Galapagos

Lips,
parched and defiant.

Sea foam trickling back
just short of you.

My heart is salt encrusted.

Dolphins and sharks kill
not half-a-mile
from your sweltering beauty.

I am black-beaded,
vigilant,
iguana.

Successful Romance

He courted disaster,
   dated delirium,
   coffeed with impetuous,
secretly longed for
               indelicata.

Women were a stream
he fished in,
to bag his mother's approval.

She dabbled with deadweight,
   danced with dark horses,
   ducked in with duplicity,
left them pondering her dust.

Men were body armor
she climbed into,
listening for the same creak as daddy.

They jumped into the same toaster,
buttered the same burnt portions,
broke down and sobbed
in each other's
tarnished reflection.

Switzerland Samadhi

Sitting on a bench in Vevey,
gazing across Lake Geneva,
the majestic Alps.

Hours pass,
I forget everything.

Another voice proclaims,
"You are eternal."

Have you ever heard something so true
you couldn't doubt it?

Once again,
"You are eternal."

Happiness spreads through me,
purest rapture.

I stand up,
a 19 year old mountain,
freed from my range.

Undertow

Heart full,
body satiated,
spirit whispering,

"No matter what, this will be received."

Drunken leaf
floating in circles
and swallowed.

Salty Sensations

In the middle of the oily boat
a salmon flings itself end over end.

The suffocating
offered up again.

Flaming lava, hot pussy,
orchids with unimaginable tongues.

What we want can't be named.

No Pockets

I am loved
this very second.

Content with this meager
now.

Standing here grinning
like a silly monk.

Wearing a robe
with no pockets.

Ko Phi Phi

Paradisiacal island in the Andaman sea,
three hour boat ride from Phukhet,
pure emerald waters arriving.

Floating on my stomach,
hands behind my back,
one with scores of
    parrot fish, clown fish, emperor angel fish,
    butterfly fish, Moorish idols, blue lined grouper,
    trumpet fish, yellow boxfish, scorpion fish,
    banner fish, orange striped trigger fish.

I give false chase,
laugh underwater,
surge and tumble
in the salty churn.

Once asleep
my body undulates
like the coral reef,
all night long.

Crazymaking

Children's screams
emigrate
from a distant schoolyard.

Tulip tunics
shrivel
under their wares.

No place to go where hardship
isn't squinting
at fierce sunshine.

Half-way 'round the world
they're bombing people
blacker than oil.

Here,
white and speckled brown,
fava beans flower.

Unstuffing

Leave the Turkey
ruffling in the wilds,
gobbling what it was created to gobble.

Thank with parsnip,
yam,
onion,
homegrown hubbard squash.

Unstuff our minds of acquisition and unholy fears.

Unstuff our violent shadow,
passing over men and women,
soldiers and parents
torn by duty and conscience.

May those who need nourishment find it.

May the one God,
who wears no uniform,
find mercy
for those who bumble in his name.

Osmosis

Drinking you in.

Melting you under
my tongue.

Touching you the way
the sea strokes
the shoreline
every few seconds.

I want you inside me
the way a toppled ginko
invites stone to replace its
woody cells one at a time
over thousands of years.

When the coyote runs,
its back paws fit precisely
into the just pressed front paw tracks.

Run with me like that.

Viva Floribunda

Pristine,
Tango,
Givenchy,
Dynasty
beckon in late summer air.

Roundelay,
National Velvet,
Shining Hour,
Arpeggio
entice,
redolent with color, scent, texture.

Perfect Moment,
Sunsprite,
Sheer Bliss,
Summer Dream,

viva floribunda[8]
and the bounty she conveys.

Blame Homer

I didn't expect
your love.

It caught me
like a right hook,
a dousing in icy waters.

The colors of your face
belong to Renoir,
to some 19th century afternoon,
warming a patrons' parlor

I didn't expect
incognito ergo sum,
sea foam sneaking confessions
across wet sand.

Elena's laden ships
plowing into one another,
mighty timbers
descending with a groan

Sunflowers

Reaching high for ennobling sun,
they stand out.

Ambitious, awkward,
clumsily demanding ordination,
big heads on spindly legs,
all too human in their proportions.

Just when they shed their green robes
for the yellow plumage of triumph,
they bow.

We know it is physics,
the burden of seed
drawing them over.
but it is something else,
a deep humility,
as if they've been touched by grace.

Bent inward like devout monks,
heavy with praise,
they turn their loveliness downward
to the cracked and parched mother
who bore them,
who barrened herself
for their eminence.

Enraptured

The nautilus curled
to hear the nuanced sea.

The bristlecone pine,
torqued four thousand years,
contorted by desert music.

The albatross slept aloft,
dreaming the sky's immensity.

The lava seethed vermillion
birthing earthen delights.

Offered

Olive-green light
soothes the Stilliguamish.

Steep generosity of lava and flies.

Identical jut of cedar trunks
await the snowy bulge.

This is what is offered.

Never Gone

Take refuge in infinite being,
peace in permanent impermanence.

Release whatever clutching
leaves you lonely.

Nothing remains but the Beloveds' desire,
and even that crushes
beautiful planets
to interstellar dust.

Today, hold nothing back.

Song for Maxfield Parrish

Start something you don't want to finish.

Rip the roof off your temple.

Lay beneath the ever-changing sky.

Tifiret[1]

Ruby tears glisten
deep inside
a pomegranate heart.

Speechless wonder.

Nowhere to go.

Something that never changed
between heaven and earth.

Footnotes

1) "ISH" means river or watershed, the home waters of native tribes that lived in the valleys of the Cascade and Olympic mountains. For example: Samish, Stilliguamish, Snohomish, Suquamish, Skokomish, Duwamish, Salish.

2) Bobby Hull played left wing for the Chicago Black Hawks hockey team throughout the 1960's. He had one of the fastest slap shots ever recorded- an amazing 118.3 mph.

3) Burma is now the republic of Myanamar. When I traveled there in 1987, the Shan province was in revolt against the national government. Gunfire rang out in the night. Quite alarmed, we asked our guide about the shooting. Grinning, he said, "Oh that, they are just hunting leopard."

4) For many years I have joyfully, danced with the Seattle Ecstatic Dance community.Their energetic, and compassionate outpourings have touched my life, and countless other lives.

5) Skookum Flats is an eight mile trail along the mighty White river, coursing down from the glaciers of Mount Rainier. "Skookum" means strong in Chinook.

6) In Buddhism, Tara is the feminine aspect of compassion that resides within all sentient creatures in the universe.

Om is the sound of the ever creating universe.
Tare means liberating from true suffering.
Tutare means liberating from fear and danger.
Ture means liberating from the ignorant of grasping of self. Soha means may the meaning of the mantra flourish in mind, body, and speech.

7) Salmonberry fruit has been an important, traditional food source for Native Americans, and is still collected today.

8) A Floribunda is a spectacular type of rose, with an inflorescence or candelabra, a spray of multiple blooms. Quite often they possess an intense and passionate fragrance.

9) Tiferet is the heart of the Tree of Life in Kabbalah. It balances giving and receiving, enabling creation to flower forth.

Author Biography
About Aaron Silverberg

Aaron Silverberg is a professional life coach, tennis teacher and father dedicated to sustaining peace and prosperity both locally and globally.

Aaron has been published in Wildheart Journal, Cascade Crest, Common Ground, Seattle Sun, Puget Sound Business Journal and Sofa Ink Press.

His previous book, "Thoreau's Chair" can be obtained at his web site www.offthemap.net

Aaron has read throughout the Pacific Northwest and often accompanies readings with his innovative flute music.

He is available for appearances and writing workshops. Please contact him at the web address above.

Thank you for purchasing this book.